ROCKS:

WE ARE DIFFERENT BUT THE SAME!
AN INTRODUCTION TO ROCKS AND MINERALS

WRITTEN BY MINNIE PONICKI
ILLUSTRATED BY LUCERO PHILLIPS

For Jenny Rupley
May she always land on an opal...

This book is dedicated to my daughter who took me out to Superior Arizona one day and reminded me how much I love digging for rocks and minerals. To all the kids out there who love learning about geology, keep the rock cycle alive!

Sometimes I am purple,
and sometimes I am
blue.

Sometimes I am yellow
with a green and reddish
hue.

I can be transparent,
or I can be opaque.

I can be solid gold or
pyrite, (which is fake).

Sometimes different crystals can make me porphyritic.

Sometimes gasses in me make me pyroclastic.

I can have different colored streaks if you give me a scratch.

I can have the same colors as others—look how we match!

Sometimes I am shiny,
and sometimes I am dull.

Sometimes I am hollow,
and sometimes I am full.

Some minerals I am made of you can often break.

Some minerals I am made of are delicate and flake.

What's different about rocks that makes us all the same?

What's a mineral, you ask—are you going to explain?

Rocks are composed of more than one mineral.

Rocks made of just ONE are minerals in general.

Sometimes I'm inside a rock, and sometimes I'm alone.

Sometimes I'm rough with lumps, and sometimes I'm a stone.

Mineral or rock, we are one big family.

Mineral or rock, come find us and you'll see.

GLOSSARY

Pyroclastic material - The volcanic rock ejected during an eruption. Pyroclastics include ash, bombs, and blocks.

Porphyritic texture - A texture of metamorphic rocks in which large grains are surrounded by smaller grained groups of other minerals.

Transparent - A material that allows light to pass through it so that things behind the material can be seen.

Opaque - Not able to be seen through.

Mineral - A solid, naturally occurring substance made of one element, with a fixed structure.

Rock - An aggregate of one or more minerals.

Stone - A rock or mineral that has been shaped and polished.

www.ingramcontent.com/pod-product-compliance
Ingram Content Group UK Ltd.
Pitfield, Milton Keynes, MK11 3LW, UK
UKRC031203030826
14089UKWH00035B/257

9798218468910